THE CENTER FOR CARTOON STUDIES PRESENTS

HARRIET TUBMAN
TOWARD FREEDOM

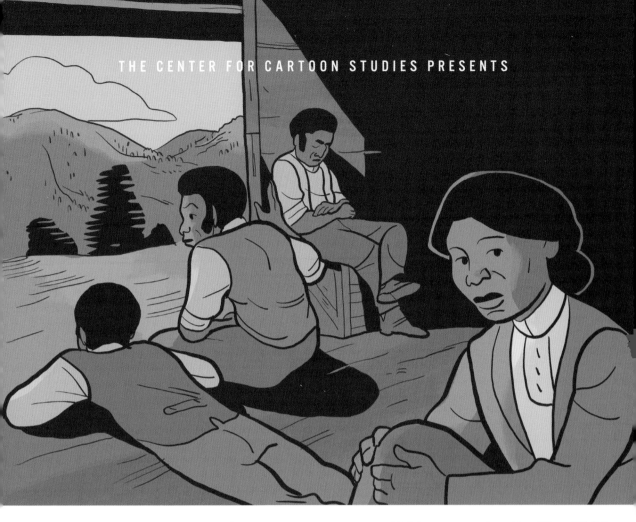

THE CENTER FOR CARTOON STUDIES PRESENTS

HARRIET TUBMAN
TOWARD FREEDOM

Whit Taylor & Kazimir Lee
With an introduction by Carole Boston Weatherford

LB
Little, Brown and Company
New York Boston

About This Book

The text was set in Adobe Caslon Pro and Felt Tip Woman, and the display type is Woodblock.

Little, Brown and Company
Hachette Book Group
1290 Avenue of the Americas, New York, NY 10104
Visit us at LBYR.com

First Edition: June 2021

Little, Brown and Company is a division of Hachette Book Group, Inc.
The Little, Brown name and logo are trademarks of Hachette Book Group, Inc.

The publisher is not responsible for websites (or their content) that are not owned by the publisher.

Library of Congress Cataloging-in-Publication Data
Names: Taylor, Whit, author. | Lee, Kazimir, 1986- illustrator. | Weatherford, Carole Boston, 1956- writer of introduction.
Title: Harriet Tubman: toward freedom / Whit Taylor & Kazimir Lee; with an introduction by Carole Boston Weatherford
Other titles: Center for Cartoon Studies presents Harriet Tubman: toward freedom
Description: New York: Little, Brown and Company, 2021. | "At head of title: Center for Cartoon Studies presents." | Includes bibliographical references. | Audience: Ages 10-14 | Summary: "Graphic biography detailing Harriet Tubman's escape from slavery and her efforts with other abolitionists to rescue dozens of those still enslaved" —Provided by publisher.
Identifiers: LCCN 2020043364 | ISBN 9780759555501 (hardcover) | ISBN 9780759555518 (trade paperback) | ISBN 9780759557666 (ebook) | ISBN 9780759555907 (ebook other)
Subjects: LCSH: Tubman, Harriet, 1822-1913—Juvenile literature. | Slaves—United States—Biography—Juvenile literature. | African American women—Biography—Juvenile literature. | Underground Railroad—Juvenile literature. | Tubman, Harriet, 1822-1913—Comic books, strips, etc. | Slaves—United States—Biography—Comic books, strips, etc. | African American women—Biography—Comic books, strips, etc. | Underground Railroad—Comic books, strips, etc. | LCGFT: Graphic novels.
Classification: LCC E444.T82 T43 2021 | DDC 326/.8092 [B]—dc23
LC record available at https://lccn.loc.gov/2020043364

ISBNs: 978-0-7595-5550-1 (hardcover), 978-0-7595-5551-8 (pbk.),
978-0-7595-5591-4 (ebook), 978-0-7595-5766-6 (ebook), 978-0-7595-5549-5 (ebook)

Printed in China

APS

Hardcover: 10 9 8 7 6 5 4 3 2 1

Paperback: 10 9 8 7 6 5 4 3 2 1

Introduction

by Carole Boston Weatherford

Besides my parents, Harriet Tubman was my first hero. I first learned about the famed leader of the Underground Railroad at my all-Black elementary school in Baltimore. I'm not sure whether the study of Tubman was required by Maryland's social studies curriculum or whether my "woke" teachers just pushed Black history (for which I'm grateful).

As a girl in the 1960s, I admired Harriet's fight. As I learned more about her, I sensed her strength, sacrifices, and spirit—the qualities that bore comparison to the biblical Moses.

Despite my early Harriet worship, years passed before I linked her to my own heritage on Maryland's Eastern Shore. One branch of my father's family hails from Dorchester County,

Tubman's birthplace, and another branch was enslaved at Wye House, the same Talbot County plantation where young Frederick Douglass first experienced slavery's brutality. These two bordering counties produced not only my ancestors but also two of the nation's leading abolitionists.

Research for my book *Moses: When Harriet Tubman Led Her People to Freedom* led *me* to Tubman's roots and to her 1869 narrative. That mythic account brought Harriet's faith into focus. For me, Harriet had become mystical and monumental.

Her legacy is enshrined in places like her former residence, the Harriet Tubman Home in Upstate New York, the National Park Service's Harriet

Tubman Underground Railroad National Historical Park, and the Harriet Tubman Underground Railroad Visitor Center and (Maryland) State Park.

Meticulously researched and visually powerful, *Harriet Tubman: Toward Freedom* chronicles Harriet's story through conversations with William Still, a Philadelphia abolitionist and a leader of the Underground Railroad. Her story begins around 1820 in Bucktown, Maryland, where she was born Araminta Ross, one of eleven children of Harriet Green and Benjamin Ross. As a child,

"Minty," as she was known, was hired out by her master. A nursemaid, she stayed awake nights so the baby would not wake the mother. If Minty nodded to sleep, the baby's mother whipped her.

From then on, Minty dreaded the lash and yearned to be free. She learned to layer clothing as padding—protection from the whip. When caught stealing a lump of sugar, Minty hid for days in a pigpen to avoid a beating. Years later, an overseer hurled an iron weight that missed its mark—an enslaved man—but hit Harriet instead. The blow crushed her skull and knocked her unconscious for days, scarring her forehead and causing seizures for the rest of her life.

After her marriage to John Tubman, a free Black man, in 1844, Minty took his last name and her mother's first name, Harriet. The marriage was short-lived, though. In 1849, Harriet decided to run away for fear of being sold. When John refused to go with her, Harriet fled with her two brothers, who both turned back. Harriet pressed on alone all the way to Philadelphia. She worked as a household servant and a cook while saving money to return to the South to help others escape on the Underground Railroad.

The Underground Railroad was dangerous business. At great personal risk, Harriet made thirteen trips back to Maryland—intent on rescuing other family members. Beyond her own kin, her bands of runaways included other enslaved people. Harriet lost patience with fearful runaways who considered returning. Knowing they would imperil others, she pulled out a gun and threatened, "You'll be free or die a slave."

As this stunning graphic novel confirms, Harriet's suspenseful saga is particularly suited to a sequential narrative. This is evident as she leads runaways from the slave-holding states to northern free states and—after the 1850 Fugitive Slave Act threatened runaways with capture and re-enslavement—as far as Canada. With a $40,000 bounty (over $1.3 million today) on her head, she used her wit to elude the patrollers.

The same grit and ingenuity that earned her the moniker "the Moses of her people" made her vital to the Union Army. During the Civil War, she served as a nurse, a cook, and a spy. She enlisted formerly enslaved African Americans to scout Confederate camps and troop movements. Armed with inside information, she joined a gunboat raid by 150 Black soldiers in South Carolina. As a nurse, she used folk remedies to treat soldiers.

After the war, Harriet continued to serve humanity in her adopted hometown of Auburn, New York, where she founded a senior citizens' home. In her later years, she petitioned Congress to receive her military pension in addition to that of Nelson David's, her late husband, a Union veteran. In 1899, Congress passed, and the president signed, legislation to increase her pension to twenty dollars a month for her service as a nurse.

Harriet emerges from this action-packed epic—pitting freedom against slavery, good against evil—as a superhero of sorts. Her deeds were legendary, but her story is not a legend. Author Whit Taylor and illustrator Kazimir Lee vividly recreate Harriet's real-life adventure from the slavery era, the Civil War, and the Reconstruction to the women's suffrage movement.

Through authentic dialogue and expressive art, *Harriet Tubman: Toward Freedom* evokes Harriet's revolutionary spirit. This graphic novel will appeal to all who pursue liberty and who push back against injustice.

The struggle continues.

—C.B.W.

'Cause how can you really know what freedom like till it yours?

I was born Araminta Ross 26 years ago in Dorchester County, Maryland.

They called me Minty for short.

I was real young when they first hired me out. Why did I have to leave my mama? I didn't understand.

I saw the suffering of my brothers and sisters.

I worked in a few houses, but I never made sense of it. We didn't choose this work.

They think our lives have no meaning but to serve their own.

Let me see, Minty.

RIIIP

When you get home, get Mama to put some ointment on it.

A couple more weeks in these fields and you'll soon have hands like me, rough and thick like leather!

Don't be scared.

It'll be your armor.

...HE also giveth.

HE told me what I need to do now, set me on this path. Mainly...

...faith in the righteousness of my mission—

constant vigilance—

communicate smart—

listen well—

be careful who you trust—

follow the plan—

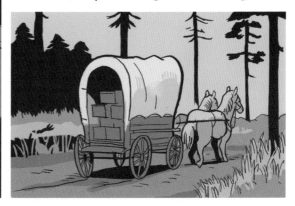

and pray that it gone be all right.

We take our orders directly from God.

1854, PHILADELPHIA.

Postal Service.

KNOCK
KNOCK

Now, wait a minute.
You a Jacob Jackson?

Yessir.

We received this letter,
addressed to you, from a William
Henry Jackson. And it's...very
curious. Any relation to you?

Ahem.

Hey, hey.

Good day, Mista Jackson. How you doing?

Boys.

Now, I coulda sworn I seen you two idlin'. Which I know your race is like to do.

UGHHH!

Drink up.

Look, I had to hire myself out tonight. This is going to be good for us, trust—

I hope this ain't the time you choose to tell me you running away again.

42

When Israel ♪
was in
Egypt's land—

46

If them slave catchers ask me, I never seen y'all.

My Minty.

60

Should stave off infection for now. Only a few more miles to go.

We almost to Delaware.

Wait here for my sign....

KNOCK
KNOCK
knock
KNOCK
knock

knock

KNOCK
KNOCK
knock
KNOCK

This is my church. And it'll be your shelter till we can get you over the bridge to Canada.

Bridge?

Yes, ma'am. Y'all heard of Niagara Falls?

What is a falls?

A waterfall?

It's sort of hard to explain but quite a sight! And it's also your best route to freedom.

A waterfall.

We almost there.

No one do at first. You'll get there, but it never fully go away. You may get a house, bear children, walk about town, "be free."

You will find something that get you up in the morning. I just know it, sis.

She's gonna come for y'all soon, Mary.

Trust, love. That freedom comin'.

HARRIET TUBMAN
TOWARD FREEDOM

Panel Discussions

PAGE 8:
William Still
William Still (1821–1902) was born in Burlington County, New Jersey, to a mother who was an escaped slave and a father who had bought his freedom. Although Still was born free, he was raised hearing about the trials of slavery from his parents. After moving to Philadelphia in 1844, Still was hired as a clerk for the Pennsylvania Society for the Abolition of Slavery and became a key figure in the Underground Railroad, helping assist fugitive slaves who came to the city. He eventually became the chairman of the Philadelphia Vigilance Committee. Still had little formal education but taught himself to read and write and used these skills to document slave stories, write letters, keep records, and unite formerly enslaved families. He is best known for his self-published book *The Underground Railroad* (1872), a documentation of the lives of escaped slaves.

During the Civil War, Still operated a post exchange at Camp William Penn, a training camp for "colored" troops, north of Philadelphia. Still became a businessman, running a stove store and purchasing a coal yard, and eventually opened the first YMCA for Blacks in Philadelphia. He was also a noted philanthropist and financier, organizing in support of civil rights for fugitive slaves and free Blacks, as well as universal suffrage.

PAGE 8: *Philadelphia Vigilance Committee*
The Philadelphia Vigilance Committee (1837–1844) was a secret branch of the Vigilant Association of Philadelphia, a group founded by abolitionist Robert Purvis (Jacob White). Like its sister organizations, the committee promoted antislavery publicly and raised funding to aid "colored" people in need through membership dues. The committee assisted runaway slaves passing through Philadelphia, providing resources such as food, clothing, shelter, transportation, medical services, and legal fees. The activities of the committee were kept private from the public to protect members, donors, and fugitive slaves from retribution.

A new General Vigilance Committee was established in 1852, with Purvis appointed as committee head. The committee focused its efforts on assisting slaves from states such as Virginia and Maryland and helping them escape to New York State and on to Canada.

PAGE 11:
Brodess Family
Rit, Harriet's mother, born between 1785–1789, was owned by a man named Atthow Pattison. Pattison's daughter Elizabeth had a daughter named Mary Pattison, who married Joseph Brodess, a Bucktown

farmer. They had a son named Edward Brodess. Mary was widowed and remarried Dorchester County landowner and widower Anthony Thompson. Mary moved into the Thompson household with her son, Edward; Rit; and four male slaves whom her deceased husband had owned. Rit met Ben Ross, one of Thompson's slaves, and they married and started a family. When Edward Brodess became an adult, ownership of Rit, Harriet, and her siblings was transferred to him. In early adulthood, Tubman and her siblings moved from Thompson's plantation to Bucktown, where Edward had his own plantation. In 1827, Edward married Eliza Brodess.

PAGE 17: *Harriet's Injury and Condition*

Harriet Tubman suffered a traumatic head injury in her youth, which affected her for the rest of her life. Historical accounts detail that she was struck with a metal weight that damaged her skull, leaving her unconscious and bloody. Tubman did not receive immediate medical care following the incident. Throughout her life, she experienced severe headaches, seizures, and bouts of narcolepsy. She was also said to have had "visions," dreams or hallucinations that she interpreted as messages from God. Some modern researchers believe her symptoms to be consistent with a temporal lobe injury, including temporal lobe epilepsy (TLE), which is associated with the sensory regions of the brain, as well as memory and emotion.

PAGE 20: *William Lloyd Garrison*

William Lloyd Garrison (1805–1879) was an influential American abolitionist, journalist, and printer-publisher. He founded the abolitionist weekly newspaper *The Liberator*, which was published from 1831 to the end of the Civil War in 1865. A fierce advocate for the emancipation of enslaved Blacks, Garrison helped organize the New England Anti-Slavery Society and founded the America Anti-Slavery Society. Garrison's strongly held beliefs, including the necessity for women's suffrage, led to a split between him and other factions of the Society leading up to the Civil War.

PAGE 22: *Fugitive Slave Act of 1850*

On September 18, 1850, Congress approved the second Fugitive Slave Act as part of the Compromise of 1850, which was designed to help settle points of contention between the North and South over slavery. Perhaps the largest expansion of federal authority over the states in the antebellum era, this law required that escaped slaves be returned to their masters upon capture. Nicknamed the "Bloodhound Law" by Blacks and abolitionists for the use of dogs to track runaway slaves, this law gave local federal officials authority in fugitive slave cases, even allowing for verdicts to be rendered without trial by jury.

The implementation of this law was met with some resistance from coalitions of free Blacks, fugitive slaves, Quakers, and abolitionists. It also led to widespread fear in northern Black communities. Enforcement of the Fugitive Slave Law led to the migration of thousands of escaped slaves from the northern United States to Canada, where they were not subject to this law.

PAGE 23: *Antislavery Bazaars*

Charity fairs became a means of fundraising along the Atlantic coasts in the 1820s and 1830s. Like bake sales, this form of fundraising was often the primary focus of women's antislavery organizations such as Ladies' Aid Societies. Bazaars, which were often held before Christmas, hosted vendors selling children's toys, sewn goods, foods, and antislavery publications. These yearly events, where holiday gifts were bought and sold commercially, led to the practice of the modern US Christmas shopping season.

PAGE 27:
Harriet's Religion
While young Harriet was required to attend Methodist church services held by her master's son Dr. Anthony C. Thompson, it is likely that she and other members of the Ross family pulled from multiple religious faiths, including Episcopalian, Baptist, Catholic, and African cultural and spiritual traditions. Tubman attended Black evangelical churches as well, such as the African Methodist Episcopal Church, which often interpreted doctrine in favor of the liberation of slaves. Black women preachers, such as Maria Stewart, Sojourner Truth, Jarena Lee, and Zilpha emerged at camp meetings on the Eastern Shore during the mid-1800s, influencing and motivating Tubman as well. It is possible that some of Tubman's hyper-religiosity was consistent with her TLE, but she drew meaning from her religious experiences and visions, believing herself to be an instrument of God who was meant to liberate and guide slaves toward freedom.

PAGE 35:
Tobacco Economy
Tobacco was a dominant cash crop in the Chesapeake region, including Maryland. Cultivating tobacco (planting, harvesting, curing, and packaging) required skilled labor year-round. Fewer slaves were required to farm tobacco compared to crops such as cotton and rice farther down south. As such, slave families in tobacco regions tended to be spread across different plantations. It was not uncommon for a husband and wife to live and work apart in "abroad marriages," with the husband being allowed to visit his children twice a week. This sort of structure led to more spread-out kinship ties compared to in the Deep South, where slave families tended to live and work together.

PAGE 41: *Breaking up Slave Families*
Slave families could be separated at any time for a variety of reasons. The domestic slave trade in the US increased with the growth of the cotton economy following the invention of the cotton gin. As a result, many slaves, particularly young able-bodied men from the upper South, were sold to plantations in the Deep South to work in the cotton fields. When slave masters died, slaves were often sold and redistributed as part of their estates. Slaves could be sold to liquidate assets and pay off debts. Slaves were "gifted" to children or as marriage presents. Mothers were often separated from their own children to care for the children of white families. Slave children were also separated for these reasons. In all cases, these separations were traumatic, causing losses of kinship, support, traditions, and culture.

PAGE 63:
Slave Weddings
Slave weddings were not legally binding or recognized during the antebellum period, although slave owners would sometimes acknowledge them for strategic reasons, such as minimizing interpersonal conflict. Slaves were aware that married couples and families could be separated at the will of slave owners at any time. Despite this, slaves still married and developed their own nuptial traditions and practices. Although the origin is somewhat unclear, one such example is "jumping the broom," where the newly married couple jumped over a broom before witnesses to bond themselves together. This custom fell out of popular practice after Blacks were able to marry legally, but it regained popularity in the twentieth century due to its portrayal in Alex Haley's book and miniseries *Roots*.

PAGE 64: *John Tubman*
John Tubman was a free Black man when he married Harriet (then Araminta) in 1844; it is not known if he was born free or acquired freedom at some point earlier in his life. Marriage between free Blacks and slaves was somewhat common along the Eastern Shore during Harriet's

lifetime, but the status of those marriages was unstable. A 1712 Maryland law stated that a child born into such a marriage would follow the status of its mother, suggesting that if Harriet and John had produced children, they would've been born as slaves. There is no official record of Harriet and John's marriage and little information on how they met, but it possibly occurred when Harriet was working for John Stewart.

PAGE 69: *Quakers*

The Quakers, a Christian denomination also known as the Religious Society of Friends, played a large role in anti–slave trade and abolitionist movements in the US and UK. In keeping with their fundamental belief that all human beings have worth and the ability to know God, many Quakers considered slavery to be immoral and unjust. Although there was some division on how to best deal with specific issues such as adherence to the Fugitive Slave Act, Quakers played a significant role in the Underground Railroad and supporting the formerly enslaved.

PAGE 84:
Niagara Falls Region

The Niagara River flows north from Lake Erie to Lake Ontario, forming a border between New York State and Ontario, Canada. This region was an Underground Railroad border-crossing location, with many available transportation routes, including through the Erie Canal and the world's first railroad suspension bridge, which operated from the mid- to late-1800s. The International Suspension Bridge (US) or Niagara Falls Suspension Bridge (Canada) connected Niagara Falls, New York, to Niagara Falls, Canada, and was able to accommodate pedestrians, carriages, and locomotives.

PAGE 94: *St. Catharines*

St. Catharines, a town located in Ontario, Canada (then the area called Canada West), was the last stop on the Underground Railroad. Since British authorities refused to extradite fugitive slaves back to the US, Canada became an increasingly popular destination for many escaped slaves after the passage of the Fugitive Slave Act. Towns such as St. Catharines provided more economic opportunity, civil rights, and protections for former slaves and free Blacks. Tubman was based in St. Catharines for ten years, supporting the resettlement efforts of escaped slaves, including family members, and participating in civic and religious life.

Story Notes

"John" was an alias of Robert, "William Henry" of Henry.

The medicines (including for pregnancy) in the story were common during that time period, but there is no evidence of what they did or did not use in these specific cases.

William Still's "sketches" were written accounts, but I chose to have him sketch images for narrative purposes.

It is not entirely clear whether Jane and Ben were already married or just engaged during their journey. I decided to portray them as married to detail slave marriage customs.

Stories suggest that John caught up with the group at the parents' fodder house, later than portrayed in this story.

The timing of Harriet's spells was added for dramatic purposes but was representative of the nature of her condition.

I took a liberty with the timing of the crossing of the suspension bridge. She did cross with a group of slaves, in 1856, but not with this specific group.

Bibliography & Suggested Reading

Bradford, Sarah. *Harriet Tubman: The Moses of Her People*. New York: Dover Publications, Inc., 2004.

Clinton, Catherine. *Harriet Tubman: The Road to Freedom*. New York: Little, Brown and Company, 2004.

Foner, Eric. *Gateway to Freedom: The Hidden History of the Underground Railroad*. New York: W. W. Norton & Company, Inc., 2015.

Larson, Kate Clifford. *Bound for the Promised Land: Harriet Tubman: Portrait of an American Hero*. New York: One World/Ballantine Books, 2004.

Lowry, Beverly. *Harriet Tubman: Imagining a Life*. New York: Anchor Books, 2008.

Still, William. *The Underground Railroad: Authentic Narratives and First Hand Accounts*. Self-published, 1872.

Credits

WHIT TAYLOR is an Ignatz Award–winning cartoonist, editor, and writer from New Jersey. She has authored many comics, including the graphic novel *Ghost Stories*, and is a regular contributor to The Nib.

KAZIMIR LEE has lived for almost equal amounts of time in Malaysia, the UK, and the US. Only mildly discouraged by the preexisting pool of talented Kazimirs in the comic industry, Kazimir adores queer and feminist subtext, ghost stories, brush pens, and pre-9/11 country music.

Series Editor **JAMES STURM** is a cartoonist and the cofounder of the Center for Cartoon Studies.

Acknowledgments

Special thanks to James Sturm for your keen editorial insights and unwavering support throughout. Thank you to Rotem Moscovich, who got us started, and Heather Crowley, who helped move us forward. Thank you to Xia Gordan for your artistic contributions in the early drafts. Thanks also to Luna Skeet Browning for your top-notch visual research and to Rebecca Dalzell for digging into the details. Thanks to Judy Hansen for all your support and to Andrea Colvin for taking the reins. And thank you, Harriet, for your courage in the face of adversity and your fight for a more just American society.

THE CENTER FOR CARTOON STUDIES (CCS), America's premier cartooning school, was founded in 2005 and is located in downtown White River Junction, Vermont. You can find it at www.cartoonstudies.org.